testimonials

"I resonated with so many of the poems. The book is a brilliant representation of the rollercoaster that is breast cancer."

Dr Liz O'Riordan
Consultant Breast Cancer Surgeon
Speaker, Author and Storyteller

"As Director of CanRehab Training, I was introduced to Dearbhaile when she attended a CanRehab Course to train as a cancer and exercise specialist instructor. During this time, she shared with the students and tutors her personal cancer journey and her desire to help those in a similar situation by delivering personalised exercise programmes. In this lovely book, Dearbhaile describes the realities and anxieties of embarking upon an exercise programme post-cancer diagnosis. This is expressed with humour and sensitivity and leaves the reader with a very positive message about the benefits of exercise after a cancer diagnosis.

I wish Dearbhaile continued success in inspiring other cancer thrivers to become and remain active and deliver the message that exercise is medicine!"

Professor Anna Campbell PhD, CEP-UK, MBE
Director of CanRehab Ltd
Chair of CanRehab Trust

An extraordinarily original take on a breast cancer self-help book. Hugely practical advice mixed with poetry, heartwrenching in one breath, and laugh out loud in the next. Not many books can be described as medically informative and humorous! It's wonderful!

Maia Dunphy
Irish Television Producer, Broadcaster and Writer

This book is a great insight into the world of breast cancer and what women and men have to go through. It would be a 'must read' for any man whose family member is going through this journey.

Reading it from a male perspective you ask yourself about male breast cancer, testicular and prostate cancer and if you should get checked.

It's a fun book at times though the subject matter isn't but I love how the poems and illustrations almost steam roll over the bumps on the road.

It's very optimistic and upbeat which is what we all want in a dire situation.

Mundy
Irish Singer-Songwriter

things went t*ts up!

trying to make rhyme and reason out of a breast cancer diagnosis.

ORLA
KELLY
PUBLISHING

All profits from the sale of this book go to support the Marie Keating Foundation
and Purple House Cancer Support

Orla Kelly Publishing,
27 Kilbrody,
Mount Oval,
Rochestown,
Cork,
Ireland.

things went t*ts up!

trying to make rhyme and reason out of a breast cancer diagnosis.

This book is written and illustrated from the hearts of two breast cancer thrivers, who the universe very serendipitously brought together to create.

A little slice of "meraki"; a Greek word to do something with soul, creativity and love; putting a piece of yourself into what you do. We hope you love reading it as much as we loved creating it!

Things Went T*ts Up is an honest and confronting expression of a breast cancer journey and takes the reader through the various stages - from self-check to diagnosis, treatment, recovery, rising and thriving and everything in between. The poems range in style from humorous and lighthearted to melancholic and touching, with the aim of educating readers, while also providing comfort and hope to anyone newly diagnosed / out the other side / living with cancer or with a loved one that finds themself in a similar position.

All profits from sales of this book with go to support The Marie Keating Foundation and Purple House Cancer Support. Please support by purchasing a copy of this book.

This book is dedicated to my gorgeous family who carried me forward on this journey, not letting my petals fall.

acknowledgements

Jess, my Kintsugi sister, thanks for sharing your story alongside mine, through your glorious illustrations.

Much love to Paul, my anchor.

Mum, Dad, Ronan and Darragh, my forever rocks.

All of my fabulous extended family, in laws, small people and friends who kept my boat afloat.

Richella, thanks for your keen eye and lifelong love.

Remembering my dear friend Róisín. My pink sister, forever in my heart.

To all the medical and oncology staff at SVPH, thanks for the second shot at this game of life.

To everyone at The Marie Keating Foundation, the world needs more people like you.

Thanks to the ARC angels, for their healing hands offering acupuncture and reflexology.

Patricia and the team at Roches, thanks for restoring my (hair) confidence and mopping up my tears of both fear and laughter.

Lisa, Sarah and the girls at Zinc, thanks for letting me blub in your salon and for your compassion and advice during my hair regrowth journey.

The Cancer Rehabilitation team at St James' Physio Department, thank you for restoring my confidence in exercise.

Robert Moore, thanks for allowing me to be part of your garden story at Bloom 2023, an experience I will never forget.

Not forgetting my fluffy companions Coco and Bowie; for keeping me entertained and active, even on those tough days.

To my employer, thanks for giving me the support, time and space to recover and heal.

Raymond Poole, thanks for proffering your wisdom on all things author-related.

Orla Kelly Publishing, thanks for helping to release this book into the wild!

David Browne, The WP Guy, thanks for your kindness and expertise.

Eileen Ireland, thanks for taking the fear out of GDPR!

Massive thanks to Goodwin and Sally – the hosts with the mosts!

table of contents

foreword

Dearbhaile,

Having just read 'Things went T*ts Up', I'm still smiling and so heartened by your beautiful words of wisdom.

Thank you so much for crafting an inspirational story out of such adversity and seeing the positivity in everything along the way. Having been on a similar breast cancer 'JoUrNeY' myself a few years ahead of you, so much of what you have described resonated with me to the core.

I am in awe of how you managed to turn such a difficult topic into something which is a joy to read and will touch your readers in a very personal and uplifting way. Your insightful description of how you faced your diagnosis through to surgery, treatments, scanxiety and post-surgery and how you are now thriving is so honest, not shirking the physical and emotional turmoil, but also shining such a spotlight of hope and courage throughout. Anyone who might hear those words 'You Have Cancer' and who reads this book will undoubtedly be more prepared for what lies ahead of them and will also take tremendous hope with them. You trusted and believed, and you DID THIS!

Thank you also to Jessica for your beautiful illustrations, which bring Dearbhaile's words to life so poignantly.

From all of us at the Marie Keating Foundation, we wish you both all the very best. We are so glad that we played a part in helping you to Survive and Thrive - we truly want to make the world a better place for those living with and through cancer.

Continue to seek out all those important little things in life and savour the magical moments every day!

Liz

Liz Yeates
CEO
Marie Keating Foundation

Part 1:
Early Days &
Diagnosis

how to do a breast check

CHECK EVERY MONTH

CHECK BREAST & ARMPIT
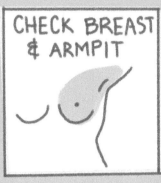

USE FINGERTIPS

UP & DOWN MOTION

WEDGE MOTION

CIRCULAR MOTIONS

LOOK FOR LUMPS

OR SKIN DIMPLING

LOOK FOR NIPPLE CHANGES

DISCOLOURATION OR LEAKS

CALL YOUR GP

feel 'em on the first

Boobies, balloons,
your wobbly bits.
Knockers, the girls,
(a bit rude to call tits!).

Some are big, some are small.
Some are flat, some are hilly.
Some can be sneaky.
Mine tried to kill me!

No matter what they are called,
we all have a pair.
And as proud owners, check in on them,
show them you care.

Examine them in the mirror.
When lying down, or in the shower.
It's better to know early.
Knowledge really is power.

Be alert for any new lumps,
rashes, puckering or peel.
Really get in there now,
have a good ole feel!

Be sure to check around your collarbones,
both boobs and under your pits.
Anywhere in the general area,
where your bra usually sits.

If you notice something odd,
make an appointment, don't delay!
Go visit your doctor
and see what they say.

If referred for a mammogram,
try not to be alarmed.
As the old saying goes,
forewarned is forearmed.

Most times it's nothing,
or perhaps just a cyst.
Buts it's vital to get checked out,
look after your bits!

On the topic of boobs,
you should now be well versed.
So set yourself a reminder,
to **"feel 'em on the first"**!

titbits

This poem is essentially the cornerstone of this book – highlighting the importance of proactively and regularly self-checking, hopefully resulting in early detection with a positive outcome.

We all need a friendly reminder to look after our bits. Knowing how and where to check are equally as important. Yes, even under your arm pits and around those collarbones! Get to know your norm and don't hang about if anything feels a bit dodgy. There is nothing to be embarrassed about and definitely don't feel like you are "wasting anyone's time". No concern is insignificant.

The wonderful team at The Marie Keating Foundation work tirelessly to provide awareness and education about the signs and symptoms of all types of cancers and to ultimately "make cancer less frightening by enlightening". Their mission is to help "create a world free from the fear of cancer". So, you see, knowledge really is power.

Please go and set yourself a reminder to "feel 'em on the first" and encourage your loved ones and friends to do the same.

Be empowered to make time for your wellness, so you are hopefully not forced to make time for an illness.

diagnosis

Despite asking the question,
I wasn't ready for this answer.
As my consultant gently tells me,
"I'm sorry, it's cancer".

There was no response
prepared in advance.
All I manage to squeeze out,
was a high pitched *"ok, thanks"*.

I'm pretty sure he was speaking,
though I couldn't hear his voice.
My brain was busy reeling,
all I heard was white noise.

There's no polite way to say it,
the next month was utter sh*te.
My body on high alert,
in constant fight or flight.

Long nights of broken sleep,
waking every hour feels rotten.
My brain playing games, reminding me it's cancer;
like I'd forgotten!

Diagnosed at the end of September,
literally means no escape.
October is International Breast Cancer Month;
I just can't catch a break.

Is it really me they said has cancer,
literally just the other day?
But I don't look or feel sick,
well not yet anyway...

I know with this downtime;
I should really be more frugal.
Instead, I do what I'm told not to,
and I consult Dr Google.

Words like "aggressive" and "critical"
start to leap off the page.
My feelings now turn from fear,
into misinformed rage.

My concentration is shot,
I stare vacantly out of the window.
My future feels so uncertain,
it's like I'm floating in limbo.

Although I can't say of hospitals,
I've ever been a fan.
But the one thing I know will give me comfort,
is to get on with a plan.

With my treatment plan laid out,
it starts to calm down my brain.
I take that giant first step of my JoUrNeY
and board the treatment train.

titbits

I think I subconsciously knew it was cancer as soon as I found the lump. But even though I half expected it, when it was confirmed and on hearing those words "you've got cancer", it was like an out of body experience. I can remember my consultant, nurse and hubby all talking, but to me it just felt like static, prickly white noise. The room started to spin and then everything just stopped. I clearly remember seeing my legs shaking, but it felt like they belonged to someone else. I really only remember two words from that appointment – cancer and treatable – and I hung onto the latter like it would stop me falling off the edge of a cliff.

The next few weeks were a slew of tests, scans and appointments - the hardest part of the entire process. Existing in limbo knowing it was "more than a lump", but not yet knowing how bad this lump was. As I was diagnosed right at the very end of September, just before October International Breast Cancer awareness month, it felt like the word "cancer" was following me everywhere. It seemed like it was the topic of every tv program, newspaper article, podcast, fund raising campaign. It was relentlessly stalking me like the dark, scary shadow on my scan.

*Even though I was
completely exhausted, both emo-
tionally and physically, I still couldn't sleep.
My brain was hyper alert, fizzing with the fear
of the unknown. Two of the scariest words I've ever
heard are "chemo" and "cancer". My every thoughts
were consumed by the "what ifs" and "buts", until all
tests were completed and we knew exactly what we were
dealing with. Once I had my treatment plan in place, a
strange calmness came over me. My fears turned into
acceptance, that it was beyond my control and I just
had to trust in the medical process and the magic
my oncology team were about to work.*

the whisper

I've something to tell you.
And I'm afraid it's not great.
I need you to be positive.
Please try keeping the faith.

My pallor is grey.
My two eyes are haunted.
Her birthday will be ruined.
By my news, unwanted.

I can't do it. I can't say it.
The words feel so wrong.
How do I tell her?
This pause feels so long.

The words won't come out.
They're tearing at my throat.
I'm sick to my stomach.
Maybe I'll just write a note?

She asks me "what's wrong love"?
I can't bring myself to answer.
Instead, he breaks the news for me.
Her only girl has breast cancer.

She holds it together.
She tells me I will be fine.
I leave the room for a breather.
Then I hear a sob and her cry.

What do we say to the others?
Will the kids understand?
Let's keep it a secret a while longer.
When I believe myself that I'll be grand.

My smile weighs a tonne,
But I wear it anyway.
I promised I'd go to this party.
So, I try it for the day.

I try to act normal.
My insides are writhing.
None of them yet know.
This heavy secret we're hiding.

A quick cry in the bathroom.
I'm losing strength fast.
I need to smile for the camera.
So, I slap on my mask.

A magic moment here captured.
Just us and a sun beam.
The exact whisper that I needed.
From my mum, my queen.

Image courtesy of Darren Maher Photography (@darrenmaher_)

titbits

Taken in October 2021, I had gone home to celebrate my Mum's birthday and God nephew's communion ... and to deliver some pretty heavy news.

I was diagnosed a few days before and barely a handful of people knew. Who to tell, what to tell, when to tell ... I really struggled with this bit.

I promised I'd be at this party, so I fixed myself up after a sneaky cry in the bathroom and wore a heavy smile for family photos. The photographer captured this beautiful moment when we were all gathering outside. A warm sunset highlighting a warm embrace.

And the whisper of encouragement from my Mum, that I so badly needed to hear at this time.

If you have any niggly nasties, please get them checked. Let this be your gentle whisper of encouragement.

wobbly strong

One minute you are wobbly
and the next you are strong.
Mixed feelings are normal,
rest assured nothing is wrong.

So many strange things,
often come as a pair.
Just like a tortoise,
racing a hare.

For every *Go* sign,
there's always a *Stop*.
And you can't have a *Flip*
without the other *Flop*.

One thing I know for certain,
none of this process is a doddle.
And every now and then,
even the strongest can wobble.

Whenever I feel a wobble,
I have a little mantra up my sleeve:
*"You can do this. You will do this.
Trust and believe".*

titbits

Wobbly yet strong. Conflicting emotions.

Being diagnosed with cancer, you are facing a pretty gruelling life challenge. Don't for one minute doubt your strength and resilience, because it is bloody enormous! You can (and will) do tough stuff.

I remember leaving the hospital on the first day of my diagnosis, feeling terrified and writing a note on my phone and saving it as a screensaver – "I can do this. I will do this. Trust and believe". This note became my little mantra whenever the going got tough.

It's perfectly normal to have more than a few wobbles throughout this JoUrNeY, you don't always have to be strong. Scream, swear and cry when you need to, but after every wobble, dust yourself off, straighten up that crown and get back to being the badass you are.

Part 2: Active Treatment

side effects

Cancer will teach you,
a whole new vocab.
Big fancy words
like Trastuzumab.

I'm handed drug info material.
It's a very long list.
Practically everything can be a "side effect".
I quickly get the gist.

There's some good and there's some bad ones,
just wait till you see.
I'll have legs smooth as butter,
but a head like a kiwi!

I didn't encounter them all,
but I did succumb to many.
Like mouth ulcers, nausea
and everything tasting like a penny.

Steroids have me both wired and tired,
with a face the shape of a moon.
Please go gentle this cycle
and hopefully this passes over soon.

You'll get through this rough time,
by following doctor's orders to the letter.
Unfortunately, it's a necessary evil,
to hopefully get better.

Most chemo drugs come with a caution,
of potential damages to your heart.
In my humble experience, they should warn you,
to never again trust a fart!

titbits

A few days before starting chemo, I was brought in to hospital to learn about the shopping list of potential chemo side effects. It made for some scary listening. Feeling suitably terrified, I was given another booklet covering some other "new to me" treatment aspects of this horrid disease, to add to the pile in the same dark drawer. Some reading for a future stage, when my brain can actually compute what's going on.

Shortly after treatment began, along came the sore bones, muscles and tendons. Nose bleeds. The scoots. Mouth ulcers. Sore nails. Sore fingers. Dog tiredness. Itchy crawling skin. Allergies to everything. And all amid chants of "but you look so well"! Don't get me wrong, I'm not complaining. At this stage I'll take a compliment anywhere I get one! Instead of being lectured on "middle age wear and tear" (post recent back surgeries), I was now delighted to be classified as being "young" (due to my age of diagnosis). Every cloud, eh?

If you are going through chemo, my advice is to speak up and self-advocate and share any nasty side effects with your team. For every side effect, there is a potential treatment. With a bit of luck on your side, chemo will go gentle and you won't experience too many from the list.

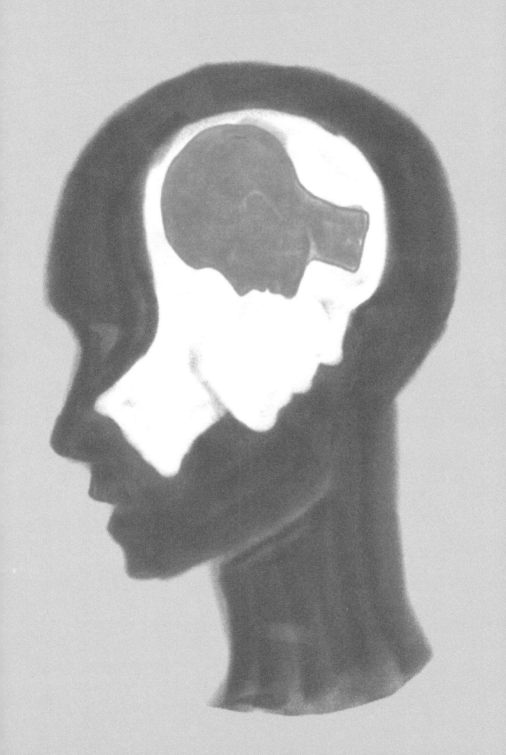

the tunnel of doom

Gowned up and nervous,
I'm led into a cold, white room.
And right there in front of me,
is the tunnel of doom.

I'm basically strapped to a surfboard,
and squeezed into a long narrow tube.
I'm surprised they don't make me lather up first,
with some sort of lube!

My mind starts to spiral,
my thoughts are a bit manic.
It bubbles up inside me,
that familiar feeling of panic.

I try to relax in this tunnel
and to calm down the swell.
My grip ever tightening,
around the emergency call bell.

The machine starts up,
with a bang and a clatter.
The room is bloody freezing
and my teeth start to chatter.

Then a contrast is injected,
into my pink IV.
It gives me a warm feeling,
like I really need to pee!

My thoughts start to race again,
just as I was getting the hang of it.
What if I get trapped in this tunnel forever,
I'll be half woman/half magnet!

I've another 30 minutes to go,
lying here in this contraption.
No time like the present,
to try the art of distraction.

So, I try some box breathing,
to see if it helps me relax.
Next time I'll cut right to the chase,
and pop a few Xanax!

titbits

Cancer comes with a smorgasbord of emotions. Scanxiety being a top tier one...whether it's anxiety about the scan procedure itself or what the scan is potentially going to show. For me, it's a bit of both really.

Firstly, those dreaded MRIs. Even just the thoughts of one now and I start to feel queasy. It's not something you "get used to". I've had lots of "practice" due to multiple MRIs and (unrelated) back surgeries pre diagnosis. It's the sheer claustrophobia element that gets me. Lying in a dark, skinny tube with your forehead brushing off the metal roof, a jackhammer in your ear and all the time thinking "what if I sneeze and knock myself out", or "what if there is a sudden power outage and I'm stuck lying here in this metal tube, for eternity, freezing my butt off". A little tip (that doesn't require prescription medication or mainlining tequila) is to put on an eye mask once you get into the room and don't look directly at the "tunnel of doom". Get in there, get on the bed and pop on the eye mask ASAP. Lie back and picture your favourite place in the whole, wide, world (mine is both feet buried in warm sand listening to the roar of the sea) and go there in your head for the next 30 mins or so. Box breathing also helps if the heebie jeebies start. Sometimes asking for talk radio to be played helps too.

As for those
weeks/days/hours/minutes
agonisingly waiting for scan results...oof.
I'm usually ok until the day of the results. Then
I micro analyse everything. "We will call you on
Friday". Ok cool, fine, no problem.

Wait, did they say ON Friday or BEFORE Friday? Friday
finally comes and I check my phone 50 times an hour
just in case they called and to ensure the battery is 100%
charged. Friday 9am comes and goes. Maybe if they call
now, it means bad news and they just want to get it over
with early. 10am passes. Ok c'mon, call me. 11, 12, 1...I
feel physically sick. What do they know that I don't know?
Maybe they leave bad news to break at the end of the day?
Actually, if that's the case, please don't call me.

Then the phone rings.

Ohmygod. Ohmygod. Ohmygod.

The tears start to flow on hearing the news. It will all be
worth it; the treatment is working.

I'm now learning to try to reduce my scanxiety by telling
myself that if something does show on a future scan,
then the experts have found the sneaky fecker
before me and can get on top of things quickly.

hair today, gone tomorrow

It's hard to be prepared,
in schools they don't teach ya.
The shock of losing your hair,
how to cope with alopecia.

It's like mourning a new loss,
you're allowed to feel some sorrow.
A full head of hair today,
but it might be gone by tomorrow.

Who knew eyebrows had a function?
How I really miss mine.
As the sweat drips down my forehead,
directly into my eyes.

I'll look on the bright side,
just think of the money I'll save.
With baby soft skin,
and legs not needing a shave.

It's all very well,
to have skin smooth as butter.
But a downside unfortunately,
is no eyelashes to flutter.

You lose hair from all over your body,
even inside your snout.
My nose is continuously dripping
as my tissue supplies run out.

Conditioners and shampoos,
all of these binned.
Instead, I hang on to my hairpiece,
during any sudden gusts of wind.

I feel vulnerable in public,
what if people stop and they stare?
It's not like I can use the excuse -
"I can't go, I'm washing my hair".

I did have an excuse once,
unfortunately, a true story...
When my dog ate my wig,
that's our dumpster dog Bowie.

Though not so funny at the time,
I now think it's a hoot.
Poor Bowie coughed up some fur balls,
after a dose of the scoots.

So, even though it's traumatic at the time,
try not to let alopecia phase you.
I promise in just a few shorts months,
you'll again be cursing your razor!

titbits

This was the bit that surprisingly hit me full force in the feels. Buying a wig while still having a full head of hair was an "experience". I didn't think the hair loss aspect would get to me so much, as I've never been blessed with thick hair, more of a fuzzy peach really! But boy did it. I think it was how "public" your diagnosis suddenly becomes and I wasn't yet ready to share my news, let alone cope with any well-meaning head tilts.

A week before starting chemo, my folks came with me to Roches to help chose a hair piece. I've always relied on them for any serious fashion decisions and we don't call my dad "Gok John" for nothing! Thankfully they were with me to help as I retreated into myself. The tears started to flow and I could barely look in the mirror while trying on wigs and hair pieces. All that went through my head during this appointment was the last time the three of us were shopping together was for my wedding dress... how life can turn so quickly.

Roughly 12 or so months later, I was back in Roches, but this time my appointment was filled with tears of laughter. I was nearing the end of my active treatment; my hair was starting to grow back and things were again looking bright. Patricia and the amazing staff at Roches fitted me in for an "emergency appointment" and sorted me out for a second time, after my "fluffy destroyer" pup Bowie had eaten my hair piece.

watch your l*ngu@ge!

Everyone has one,
a word or phrase that they hate.
It gives you the ick when you hear it,
on every nerve it will grate.

Language is confusing;
Because it's always evolving.
It's very easy to cringe,
by saying the wrong thing.

When it comes to cancer language,
we are all constantly learning.
Take for example,
personally, I hate the word "JoUrNey"!

And while we are at it,
don't get me started on "BaTtLe".
No one "LoSt" theirs,
that just meaningless prattle.

If you are stuck for words,
whatever you do don't answer...
With at least you got the
"GoOd TyPe of CaNcEr".

And please never let the following words
spill from your gob.
"Sure, aren't you LuCkY to be getting
a Free BoOb JoB".

It's always lovely to meet up,
for a walk and a chat.
Just refrain from mentioning
"My GrAnDmA DiEd FrOm ThAt".

Switch off from social media,
if you come across those chancers,
peddling untruths and rubbish
like "SuGaR fEeDs CaNcEr".

To *you* it might be insignificant
and *you* might not even care.
But to *them* it could be traumatic,
it's not "OnLy JuSt HaIr".

Whether you are sporting a new wig
or rocking a head shave.
The last thing you want to hear is
"Gosh, you're so BrAvE".

Sometimes it's best just to listen
and if ever in doubt,
Remember there's a reason we all have 2 ears
and only 1 mouth!

titbits

This poem is very tongue in cheek, but these are a few of the irksome phrases shared by fellow thrivers while BaTtLiNg their JoUrNeYs!

You may have noticed me writing the word JoUrNeY throughout this book as such...it took me a good 12 months to tolerate this word, without it feeling like nails scratching on a chalkboard! To me, a "journey" implied a passport, sun loungers, pina coladas, salty lips and sandy toed adventures...not quite what panned out here! And personally, I didn't feel very BrAvE at all; I don't think I have been more scared in my life than those first few weeks after initial diagnosis!

Of course, everyone means well and ultimately wants to share any little nugget of advice they think might help. Understand that everyone is saying these things out of kindness and remember you are walking your own unique path.

It is also good for us all to acknowledge that not everything "happens for a reason" in life, some things are just really sh*tty and should never have happened.

If you are ever unsure of what to say to someone with cancer, or anyone facing any of life's many challenges, just be that special heart that listens.

brain freeze

Having experienced the cold cap,
a scalp cooling system.
Let me try to impart,
a few words of wisdom.

You will need to dig deep,
try to grin and to bear it.
After 10 minutes you'll adapt.
Honest, I swear it!

Allow an extra hour, maybe two,
to freeze and defrost.
But it's definitely worth a try,
to hopefully slow down chemo hair loss.

Though I didn't go completely bald;
I was more like Friar Tuck.
Thankfully a new hat collection,
helped me pull off my new look!

So, if you chose the cold cap,
remember grit your teeth at the beginning.
Just try to visualise yourself,
in the Irish sea swimming.

titbits

At my first Oncology Medical appointment, my wonderful oncologist gently persuaded me to give the cold cap a go. I'm so glad I did. It's not a guarantee for everyone, but it can even perhaps help ease you into the idea of hair loss. Some people immediately embrace and brave the shave, while others might choose the cold cap (if it's suitable). Like everything to do with a cancer diagnosis, you will walk your own path.

I won't lie, the cold cap does take a little getting used to and you do need to add on about an hour either side of your infusions. My top tips are to invest in "Simple" conditioner, a wide-tooth comb and a head band. Bring these along to each appointment to help with the cap fitting. The night before my first chemo infusion, we drove around every Boots shop in Dublin looking for "Simple" condition. Eventually we found it in stock and I bought a six pack (of conditioner that is, though I really could have done with it being beer at that time!).

The first 10 mins of "cold capping" are tough. It felt like a tight, ice-cream headache and gave me flashbacks of winter dips in the Irish Sea! But once you get through those initial minutes, your head is basically numb and you won't feel much more discomfort. Lots of fluffy blankets, cosy sock, heat packs and woolly hats will pull you through. Fun fact - you will need to defrost after your session. Literally. I remember feeling the icicles crunching in my hair

*each time I removed
the cap! Using the cold cap
meant I did get to keep some of my hair,
which also meant I could use clip in hair pieces
right the way through my treatment and beyond.
In fact, those hair pieces looked so much better than
my own hair ever did and saved me a fortune on
highlights! Luckily, I started chemo in winter so many a
beanie was bought to hide my Friar Tuck head if out in
public!*

*The pic here is of my first chemo infusion using the cold
cap for the first time. I look a bit like a frightened jockey!*

neulasta

Another surprise was a jab,
I hadn't expected.
To be administered post chemo,
within 48 hours as directed.

You better not forget it;
this is not the time for amnesia.
It's important to keep well
and prevent neutropenia.

Which is a fancy way of saying,
don't forget to take this injection.
The last thing you want right now,
is to get an infection.

It's stored in the fridge;
Amgen make it in their lab.
You'll quickly get used to
administering this jab.

First, remain calm,
don't do this while rushing.
No one wants to resemble
a human pin cushion.

Take it out of the fridge
and inspect the prefilled syringe.
If you warm it with your hands first,
it won't hurt, it's more of a twinge.

Wash your hands thoroughly,
then prepare the injection site.
Your upper arm or your belly,
My preference was a juicy thigh!

The injection is the main course.
Unfortunately, there's a common complaint.
It comes with a few drawbacks,
one being a side dish of bone pain.

It's really not so bad though,
in fact, it's over in a jiffy.
Hopefully you'll feel fine after your shot.
Perhaps sometimes just a bit squiffy.

The aim of this poem is to teach you,
how to safely inject yourself with Neulasta.
To help keep you free from infections,
and let your white cell count recover faster.

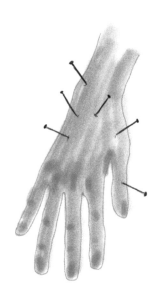

titbits

Chemo is great at fighting cancer, but it also puts you at high risk of infection. The last thing you want is to delay your treatment plan, in so far as possible. Every 3 weeks I silently pleaded "just get me in that chair and get another infusion off the list"!

Neulasta is a brand name for pegfilgrastim, a prescription medicine that is given once per (certain) chemo cycles, to help to reduce the chance of infection due to a low white blood cell count. In fancy pants terms, it helps prevent neutropenia by activating and releasing neutrophils from the bone marrow to increase white blood cell counts, which are crucial in fighting infection. Like many a thing mentioned in this book, I'd never heard of it before diagnosis.

You will be taught by a health professional how to administer the injections at home. My two top tips are (1) alternate the injection site each cycle (left side, right side) and (2) take it out of the fridge 30 mins before injecting yourself and warm the syringe in your hands first. This takes the stingy ouch factor away!

a few of my (least) favourite things

Biopsies feel like your boobs have been bitten.
Bags filled with chemo, I bid you good riddance.
Hospital gowns -- tied up with strings.
These are a few of my least favourite things.

Reading scary info -- on Dr Google.
New chemo curls, make me look like a poodle.
Another damn infusion -- and the canula stings.
These are a few of my least favourite things.

Docs in white lab coats and blue scrubs with sashes.
Losing both eyebrows and then my eyelashes.
Painful joints -- and tingly limbs.
These are a few of my least favourite things.

When the fatigue hit!
When my mouth hurts!
When I'm feeling sad!
I simply remember my favourite things.
Like when this is over, I'll be so glad!

titbits

I think I was feeling a bit fed up of it all when I wrote this! It reads more like "The Sound of Losing It", than "The Sounds of Music".

A classic case of "Fedupitis".

Enough said. Enjoy the earworm!

sisters not twins

Trying to dodge Covid before surgeries,
felt like playing Russian roulette.
The sooner I got on with it, I'd get over it,
was my mindset.

The day finally arrived
and I checked myself in.
Not quite the holiday I'd planned,
my head in a spin.

I'm injected with a radioactive dye,
then to the waiting room I'm shown.
I start to nervously giggle,
when I read the sign saying "hot zone".

I'm marked up with a pen,
from my navel to my neck.
I start to resemble a sewing pattern,
from Leaving Cert Home Ec.

I walk into theatre,
not the most dignified of struts.
Clutching at my blue gown,
that's exposing my butt.

The theatre lights are so bright,
they would practically blind you.
A nurse gently whispers,
"don't worry I'll mind you".

There's a flurry of blue scrubs
and a hum of rhymical beeps.
And just like that,
I drift right off to sleep.

Next thing I know,
I'm awake from my slumber.
With drains and a surgical bra.
A far cry from Anne Summers!

After a week in hospital,
I quickly lost count.
More people had seen Perky
than if she had an Only Fans account!

Unfortunately, due to an infection,
Perky had become quite the attraction.
Each time my room door opened;
I lifted my top, like Pavlov's reaction!

It was just out of pure habit;
I promise I wasn't being shady.
And I apologized profusely,
to one very shocked tea lady!

Perky will never match Pamela,
of that there's no doubt.
The girls are now sisters, not twins,
one more north, one more south!

titbits

A mastectomy is not a free boob job!

Ok, I've got that off my chest now (pun intended!). Whether it's a single or double mastectomy, lumpectomy, reconstruction, implant, flap, flat, whatever - it's a big deal. It's a major change to the body you have lived in all your life and will take some time to get used to again. Just don't expect miracles of perfect symmetry, but instead savour the massive, glorious relief that the sneaky fecker is now gone.

I think you can always find humour, even during dark moments. Two vivid and funny memories during my surgical hospital stay were "the hot zone" and "balloon gate".

Before sentinel node surgery, a radioactive tracer substance is injected near the tumour, so the surgeon can then detect your sentinel lymph nodes during surgery. It's not the best craic really, but a necessary evil. I remember being guided to the radionuclide imaging waiting room and having a giggle to myself when I noted the sign above saying "hot zone". I still kick myself that I didn't have my phone with me to take a selfie to add here!

During the week of my surgery stay, visitors were not allowed due to Covid restrictions. My hubby did get a special dispensation for a short visit once during my stay, but it still meant for long days and lonely nights. Being on the 6th floor did come with a little bonus though. There were some amazing views of the summer sunsets casting a golden hue across the beach nearby every night, each one promising me a brighter tomorrow. A few nights after my surgery, a security man knocked on my door around 9pm (I kept my top down, honest!). He floated in carrying a massive pink helium balloon, with the news that there were 4 more outside! Suitably mortified, I didn't know what to do with them, so I hid them in the shower in the bathroom and pulled the shower curtains around them. A poor unsuspecting nurse came in to help empty my grenades (drains) later that night and got the land of her life when she went into the bathroom! It gave a whole new meaning to people coming into my room to check out my balloons!! Then there was the walk of shame on discharge, me carrying 5 massive pink helium balloons, each with my name emblazoned on them, just in case I was trying to be in any way discrete during my not so subtle and dignified exit! Equally as funny was my hubby trying to squeeze them into the boot of his car in the hospital car park!!

Thanks for reframing memories from painful to joyful Annabel and I'm still plotting my revenge moves!

exercise is medicine

It's like winning the lottery,
in fact, it's better than wealth.
To be in the full of your senses,
with good mind and body health.

After a cancer diagnosis,
they both take a hit.
As part of your recovery,
you need time to get fit.

It's not about a bikini bod,
or having perfect form.
It's to be healthy and happy
and ultimately stronger than your storm.

The goal is to feel well,
while learning a new skill.
Hopefully replacing some of your medicines,
with time on a treadmill.

They say it's good for the heart,
and it's also good for the head.
It's great for routine
and gets you up out of bed.

It stretches your muscles
and it strengthens your bones.
It's clears out your mind
and gets you off those damn phones!

So, I squeeze into my Lycra,
and dust off my gym shoes.
I say goodbye to my wobbly bits,
hopefully soon to be yesterday's news!

How I wish there was a safe space to work out,
where no one would care.
As I rock up to the gym, wrapped in Lycra,
with one boob and no hair.

Unfortunately, this time,
my fears weren't abated.
I'm surrounded by gym bunnies,
and feeling totally "gymtimidated".

I meet with my trainer,
He's perfectly sculpted like a T-bone steak.
I feel like an imposter, an alien,
I'm truly a fake.

Trying not to feel self-conscious,
or silly or stupid.
It boils down to the simple fact,
"If you don't move it, you lose it".

After the slightest exertion,
I'm already out of puff.
Unfortunately, my current physique
is more buffet than buff.

It feels like hell right now,
but tomorrow I'll be glad.
When I begin to feel muscles,
I never knew I even had.

I mount an exercise bike,
and elegantly throw over my leg.
I'm sure I've a six-pack hiding in there somewhere,
it's just buried deep under a keg!

I build up a sweat,
as I stifle my giggles.
How I wish I had eyebrows,
to catch all the dribbles!

I get down on the mat,
to try something called a burpee.
I manage about 5,
even though the instructor said 30.

20 jumping jacks later,
I'm hotter than hell.
As I'm handed some yolk,
he called it a kettle bell.

He tells me to squat,
with my kettle bell a swinging.
I'm already pooped and it's just the warm up
...the class is only beginning!

I survive all 40 minutes,
thankfully it wasn't any longer.
This marks the beginning of my come back,
and I vow to come back stronger.

I'm now a regular gym goer.
In fact, I've got an annual subscription.
I'm living proof that exercise is medicine,
just without a prescription!

titbits

Exercise and movement have played such a fundamental part in my tolerance of chemotherapy / immunotherapy regimens, recovery from surgeries and infusions and overall survivorship. As cancer patients, there are so many aspects of our treatment plans that are out of our control, but through movement and exercise we can take back some control and reap the immeasurable mental and physical rewards.

Having experienced back surgeries pre diagnosis, I already had first-hand experience of how quickly your mobility can be taken away. It's exactly like that saying "if you don't use it, you lose it". So, with this in mind I set myself a challenge of walking 10k steps every day throughout my cancer treatment and to take a photo of something unusual and beautiful on each of my daily walks. This gave me a routine (outside of the numerous hospital appointments), helped me to have a daily focus and to stay as mentally and physically strong as I could, throughout my treatment and beyond. It also taught me to slow down and appreciate the little things and I have an added bonus of some lovely photos to look back on!

As soon as I got clearance after my surgeries, I was keen to get back to the gym, to start rebuilding confidence, strength and flexibility and ultimately to come back stronger! I considered myself so lucky to be able to exercise, simply because I could. ("Because I can" became another one of my little mantras.) When going through chemo/immunotherapy, you start to notice a pattern to your weeks...they generally start out with you bursting with energy from the steroid high, then the wheels start to fall off a bit and then day-by-day you start to feel a bit better, before the next cycle starts all over again. I used this pattern to plan in what felt right for me on any given day, from gentle movement and stretching, to more strenuous exercise.

I fully appreciate that it is hard enough to drag yourself to a gym when you are in the full of your health, but when you are at your most vulnerable, the last thing you need to feel is "gymtimidation". A wonderful physio took me under her wing for some medically supervised strength training classes in a hospital gym setting. This meant a safe and fun space to work out, with no one caring if I was wearing a wig or had wonky boobs, just each of us showing up to do even the gentlest of movement if it was a particularly "bad day" (and there were some). It also took me a while to realize that on my "good days" I could push myself (while under physio/medical supervision) when it came to exercise during my cancer treatment. After completing my first full strength and conditioning class post-surgery, I actually felt very emotional. Exercise made me feel like me again.

Rather than the old school thinking of wrapping ourselves in cotton wool during treatment, I think as patients, we need to be made aware of the importance of moving through cancer, and guided safely with the knowledge and confidence to make daily movement a lifelong habit. Having a chronic condition, can still equate to living a healthy, fulfilling life! Currents Irish statistics show that one in nine women and one in 1000 men will develop breast cancer in their lifetime. There are currently more than 2500 breast cancer survivors living in Ireland. With all types of cancer survivorship on the rise and the continuous emergence of new life-saving therapies, I truly believe that "exercise is medicine", whether that's prehab to prepare you for surgery/treatment, or rehab during and post treatment and on into survivorship.

I hope this little poem, in some small way, can inspire any fellow cancer patients to get moving through your treatment (even on the darkest days) and empower you to come back stronger, after the fight of your life.

... "because I (know you) can".

one last little drop

19 long months,
mapped out in 3-week blocks.
How surreal today feels,
with these few remaining drops.

Goodbye surgeries, side effects,
and bags filled with chemo.
Pinch me and wake me.
If I'm dreaming, please say so.

The outpouring of love,
has felt like a cosy embrace.
You've all made this bumpy JoUrNeY,
so much easier to face.

I'm eternally grateful,
now my active treatment is almost a wrap.
Much love to you all,
right to the moon and then back.

Bubbling up with emotion,
not knowing whether to laugh or to cry.
19 months of treatment almost over,
in the blink of an eye.

Though the feelings are raw,
I really couldn't be happier.
Time to turn the next page
and to start a healthy new chapter.

This split second in time,
Marks the moment my active treatment will stop.
As I begin my recovery,
after this one last little drop.

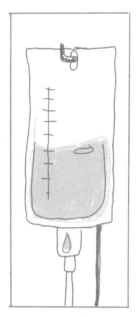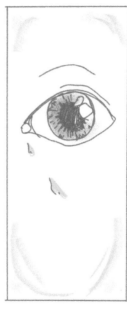

titbits

I wrote this poem sitting in the chemo chair during my *fingers crossed* last chemo infusion. It was a quiet but powerful moment of celebration. The significance of seconds really struck me. One last second and this one last little drop were all that were separating me from being a "cancer patient" to a "cancer survivor".

19 months, 25 chemo infusions, a few surgeries, countless scans, some bumps in the road, a river of tears, who knows how many needle sticks and innumerable pills...I'm still here.

Relieved, hopeful, tearful. Grateful, proud and alive.

For the first time in a long time, I now have hope again, for a future that will happen. I start to think and plan further than 3 weeks ahead.

I look forward to dreaming into the distance.

two little words
(with a very big meaning)

How can just two little words
even suffice?
When the care and expertise given,
basically, saves someone's life.

Where do I even start?
There's such a long list.
Surgeons, oncology, radiology,
the friendly phlebotomist.

While on the topic of ologists,
there's been quite a few.
Rheumatologist and endocrinologists,
I've had more visits than the zoo!

Plastic surgeons and nurses,
stitching and picking up all of my pieces.
Not to mention the pharmacist, filling my prescription,
the size of a thesis.

A special shout out to my GP,
a legend like no other.
I'm so lucky and blessed,
he's also my fabulous big brother.

My wonderful hubby and family,
four legged companions and neighbours.
Colleagues and friends coming to my rescue,
each providing favours.

Hairdressers not charging,
while offering to do a head shave.
The Marie Keating Foundation and ARC,
showing me how to thrive and be brave.

Not to mention the new bonds,
instant connections made with survivors.
Always offering an empathetic ear,
and a strong shoulder to cry on.

The ladies at Roches
also need to be part of this gig.
For sorting me out last minute,
after my pup ate my wig!

The stream of WhatsApp's and texts,
a tsunami of love.
Candles you've lit,
offering prayers to the man up above.

Everyone mentioned,
in their own special way have been lifesavers.
It's overwhelming and beautiful,
even the kindness of strangers.

I apologise profusely,
if there's someone that I may have missed.
Let me sneak one last person in,
my lovely physiotherapist.

Just two little words,
each holding a meaning almost as big as "I do".
I'm eternally grateful to each and to all,
so, here's a massive THANK YOU.

titbits

What can you possible say, that they haven't already heard...having done so much for me, that truly means the world?

Aside from the support and care from my amazing oncology team at St Vincents Private Hospital (SVPH), I am blessed to be surrounded by a gorgeous family, circle of friends, colleagues and neighbours. The support I received throughout my treatment felt like a tsunami of love. Cards, flowers, books, woolly socks, rude embroidery, chocolates, cakes. Balloons! Even earphones, Crème de la Mer and a glorious sparkly handbag...the utter extravagant fanciness of it all. So much so, I though, gosh I must really be sick to be getting this level of fancy!

Every single phone call, card, text message and WhatsApp meant the world to me and lifted me up on reading.

One of my favourite texts was from my Dad, on the morning of my first chemo infusion, wishing me luck. It included a picture of Coco (my parent's dog) jumping and chasing "holy bubbles from Knock". It warmed my heart then and still does today!

I am eternally grateful to all who have worked their medical and supportive magic, helping me come out the other side.

THANK YOU all for my fresh start and my very full heart.

Part 3: Recovery

all at sea

How should I feel,
after being finally released,
From the clutches and jaws
of the cruel cancer beast?

No rule book for this phase,
I feel like a dunce.
As I'm waved on from Oncology
with a "see you in three months".

My mind was busy with appointments,
this safety net now gone.
Surely, I should be elated,
when finally freed to move on?

"Woman up" I tell myself,
not everyone gets second chances.
It's down to pure luck,
and thankfully medical advances.

So, I pick up my oar
and paddle right out to sea.
Is this what it's meant to feel like,
what they mean by recovery?

Waves of anxiety,
crash over my small rowing boat.
Please throw me a lifeline, anything,
just keep me afloat.

I'm feeling all at sea,
so alone and afraid.
My cry for help heard,
by a lonesome mermaid.

She says *"there's always a rainbow,
after each and every storm"*.
Now's my time to figure this out
and discover my new norm.

She tells me *"Things will be different,
just never the same as before"*.
And she helps steady my boat
and I row slowly back towards the shore.

titbits

As grateful and oh so lucky as I am to reach the end of active treatment, it's been kinda scary too. Initially, I felt like I had been released back into the wild after months in captivity!

I've learnt that healing is a process. It takes its sweet time. You need to take your time to adjust to what you now consider your "new normal". At the beginning, I felt a little lost, but as promised, slowly I've started to feel strong again. The old spark does return! This is only one chapter in your book of life and as Dermot Kennedy sings, "better days are coming".

Something a friend said to me when I was first diagnosed, was that there is always a rainbow after a storm. This stuck with me as it was such a lovely, comforting thing to hear at such a scary and vulnerable time.

If you are struggling, just remember that your storm will pass. It just might take a little while to dry out after. Chin up, dry off, readjust your crown and keep chasing those rainbows.

as the dust settles

With treatment finally over,
it felt like processing a bereavement.
My poor mind pummelled with info,
and body pummelled by treatment.

Catapulted into a club,
I never asked to join.
Now comes the time,
when I need to move on.

When I finished my active treatment,
I thought I'd feel elated.
Instead, I just felt...
utterly discombobulated.

Having counted down the days,
until active treatment would end.
Only for my mind to then start yelling
"What the hell has just happened?".

I'm learning that recovery
takes both strength and fragility.
And a very large dose
of bounce-back-ability.

It will take time to move forward
and to find my new level.
Now the tornado has passed,
and the dust starts to settle.

titbits

As recovery is often a stage overlooked and one so many of us struggle with, I thought it deserved a second poem!

My advice is to keep yourself busy doing things you truly enjoy. Be kind to yourself. Be patient with yourself. Give your brain and body the time it needs to move on from "fight or flight" to "forgive and (hopefully) forget". You are stronger and even more resilient that you realise. You are enough.

the niggles

Some say monsters live in your closet,
or hide under your bed.
When actually the scariest place they can hide,
is inside your head.

We all have our monsters;
I call mine the Niggles.
They creep up really slowly
and steal away my giggles.

They feed on the "what's if's"
and they gorge on the "buts".
So, it's my job to starve them
and drive the Niggles a bit nuts!

They thrive when it's scan time,
there's nothing juicer than results.
They mess with my thinking,
and even elevate my pulse.

These Niggles could give Dr Google
a run for his money.
Convincing me it's a tumour,
not just a pain in my tummy.

They tell me every ache is serious,
and bound to be fatal.
The Niggles are meanies,
they truly are hateful!

They sit on my shoulder
and whisper quietly in my ear ...
*"It could come back you know,
there's always that fear".*

I'm learning to stop feeding the Niggles
and instead to think of something nice.
Lightening, can do,
but rarely strikes twice.

Together we can fight off these Niggles
and put an end to their torment.
By forgetting the past and the future
and just living in this moment.

titbits

*This poem is ultimately about the fear of recurrence.
There's a childish lilt to this poem. It reminds me of when
my mum (a retired GP) used to say "when sick, treat adults
like children and children like adults".*

*Its ok to feel scared, even as a "grown up". Sit with these
feelings for a while and then move on from them. Try
your best to leave the past behind you.*

Right here, right now, is what really matters.

menopause

Just as you reach middle age,
when life should be for living.
Along comes the menopause,
the gift that keeps giving!

What age will it start,
is anyone's guess.
It usually creeps up slowly,
with those awful night sweats.

Anxiety, confusion,
the dreaded brain fog.
A list so long,
you end up keeping a log.

My middle gets fatter,
it's my hair that gets thinner.
Not one bit of menopause
feels like a winner.

It's not only bad,
it's actually worse than I was fearing.
All I gain is more weight,
as I lose my eye sight and hearing.

Am I the only one that feels
like a big old weirdo?
And while I have your attention,
has anyone seen my libido?

Deep lines on my forehead,
around my eyes and my mouth.
Any bits that were north,
now droop and hang south.

Please Mother Nature,
can't you just leave me be.
And who do I have to bribe
to prescribe some HRT?

If I knew what would help,
I'd be all over it like a rash.
But I'm just flat out busy,
trying to control the next hot flash.

Please God, give me a break,
and just leave my body alone.
But instead of giving me strength,
He decides to weaken my bones.

I tell myself I'm not going crazy
and that things will be grand.
Says she who uses the torch on her phone,
to search for the phone in her hand!

No one should put up with this,
in fact, it should be against the law.
Just as you think things are safe,
then comes that last straw...

"Relax" says he.
"Sure, it's only a phase".
Then a red mist descends,
beware of menopausal rage!

titbits

I have a newly acquired, special talent, whereby I often forget what I'm doing, right while I'm doing it! Like searching for my phone to look something up while speaking to someone on it; or pulling the house apart looking for my glasses, that are resting on top of my head; or walking into a room to get something I've already forgotten about; or forgetting names of people I've known half of my life or the right word for everyday objects...! Not to mention my daily ponderings of "is it hot in here or is it just me?".

Whether it happens naturally, or you are propelled there chemically or surgically, menopause is a fact of life. Unfortunately, depending on the type of your breast cancer, HRT may never be an option for you. But there's still lots of help and support available out there and also lots of things we can empower ourselves to do, from movement to nourishment and everything in between.

Not to bang on about it again, but strength training really is so good for us ladies, particularly at this stage of life. Not just to strengthen our bones, build our muscle mass and increase our energy levels, but also to give us the confidence and fierceness to age like a badass.

me before c

Energetic, unbreakable,
naive and carefree.
Words that best describe,
the pre-cancer me.

Tired, a bit broken,
vulnerable, sometimes angry.
Words that best describe,
me after big C.

Who *was* she? Who *is* she?
Who *will* she be?
Sometimes it's difficult to remember,
the me before C.

In Japanese culture,
they mend broken things with flair.
They call this art "Kintsugi",
or "golden repair".

Smashed items are repaired,
with a glue made of gold.
Fixing broken things back together,
repairing them even more beautiful than before.

Us Irish have a word for strength.
A Gaelic word called "neart".
I'm grateful for the strength to fight my battle,
and my newly gold-plated heart.

titbits

Conflicting emotions often coexist.

Like grief and gratitude. Heartbreak and healing.

A breast cancer diagnosis is a pretty life-changing event. It is a cruel disease and can be heartbreaking in so many ways. Whether we are grieving the loss of our old selves, our hair, fertility, body parts or the excruciating loss of a loved one, it sucks.

But there is gratitude and healing that happens along the way too.

I've always loved the concept of the Japanese art of Kintsugi...taking shattered vessels and lovingly repairing them even more gorgeous and stronger than before.

And as Leonard Cohen so eloquently put it; "There is a crack in everything, that's how the light gets in".

the black horse

Vibrant pink hair
and eyes the colour of water.
Her whole life revolving
around her beautiful daughter.

Such strength and resilience,
an absolute fighter.
So full of sparkle,
making everyone's day brighter.

She bore her long illness
with dignity and grace.
Always a spring in her step
and warm smile on her face.

Supporting the pink cause,
was her true passion.
She was a beautiful pink rose,
a dedicated follower of fashion.

She oozed with style
and always with a touch of class.
Billie, Jack and Ziggy
were her beloved house cats.

Our friendship spanned 16 years,
it feels surreal.
Considering we first bonded over a car,
that we christened the Batmobile!

A ribbon tattoo on her wrist
and a bejewelled earlobe.
With her beautiful daughter,
together they travelled the globe.

From Thailand to West Cork,
together they strayed.
Ensuring many precious
and everlasting memories were made.

Instilled within her,
a love of music and dance.
She used to day dream of Jack L
or a Bowie romance!

She fought the good fight,
never once giving up hope.
She won many battles,
The strongest person I've known.

How she wished from her illness,
she could be set free.
She sought solace in her garden
and was happiest by the sea.

A firm believer in the meaning
of when robins appear.
*"When you see one in the future,
know that I'm near"*.

Unfortunately, the time had come,
for her to finally let go.
"Don't leave me my friend,
please say it isn't so".

Pulled away from this world,
with such brutal force.
My beautiful friend left us,
riding her black horse.

The pain of loss,
the depths of this sorrow.
"Goodbye Róisín. I love you;
I'll see you tomorrow".

titbits

I know not everyone is fortunate enough to receive treatment with curative intent. Unfortunately, the harsh reality is nearly each and every one of us has suffered the loss of a loved one from some form of cancer.

To acknowledge the darker shade of pink and with the blessing of her beautiful daughter Darcey, I'm sharing here a poem I wrote a few days after my friend Róisín's death on September 7th 2022.

A black horse is a spiritual meaning that symbolizes endurance, strength, and perseverance. Signalling difficult times ahead, it is encouragement to push on in the face of adversity. I thought this a fitting title for this poem, as when I think of Róisín's death, I see her galloping off on her black horse. I was lucky to visit Róisín in the hospice just hours before she mounted her black horse and I got to tell her I loved her and to thank her for being such an amazing friend. My last words to her were "I'll see you tomorrow".

I first met Róisín 16 years ago when I bought my first car from her. She was heavily pregnant at the time and could no longer fit her expanding bump into a tiny sporty Smart Coupe. I was feeling newly minted (!) with my SSIA savings and used these to buy this car from her, despite the small fact that I couldn't yet drive. This car, affectionately known as "The Batmobile" was the start of a wonderful and treasured friendship. Things have come full circle and "The Batmobile" now belongs to that same beloved bump, a 3rd proud owner, Róisín's adored and treasured Darcey! A lovely circle of life.

When someone has gone, I think it's important to remember that you can keep part of them alive in your heart; with your memories, words and actions. Speak their name, greet those robins, collect those feathers, listen to those whispers in the wind and delight in those rainbows.

Part 4:
Rising &
Thriving

the fierce phoenix

Three little words,
no one wants to hear.
Those three little words
that can strike such fear.

First come the scans
and waiting for the answer.
Then you hear those three words;
"You've. Got. Cancer".

My body goes numb
and the room goes so quiet.
As laid out before me
is the fight of my life.

Weighed down with appointments
and a whole new vocab.
...Taxotere, Carboplatin,
Perjeta, Trastuzumab.

An emotional rollercoaster,
complete with turns and twists.
And a host of nasty side effects,
longer than Santa's naughty list!

More surgeries and results,
another nerve-wracking wait.
Keep the head down. Keep calm.
And try keeping the faith.

Some welcome hair regrowth,
as I ditch the cold cap.
Will I need radiotherapy
for that reassuring extra zap?

One year on from diagnosis,
I'm still very much alive.
Not only that,
I fully intend to thrive!

Logging on each week
for us thrivers to vent.
Some even admitting to
the odd "Snaxident"!

We are now armed with a "tool box"
that would make Bob the Builder blush!
And a bottom shelf in the fridge,
that no longer turns to mush!

Weekly "action plans" are formed,
with pledges to squeeze in more fruit.
Amid the chants of *"What's that you said there,*
I think your mic is on mute!"

With all the promises we make,
to eat greens with each meal,
And at the rate we are all walking,
we will have buns made of steel!

Lots of tips shared,
to help with emotions and decision making.
Along with a prescription,
for some weekly nature bathing.

We are all reassured,
that following the food pyramid becomes easier.
As I daydream of future holidays
and visiting the pyramids in Giza!

Six short weeks later,
us thrivers wish it was longer.
Swapping our red wine for water,
we each vow to **Come. Back. Stronger.**

We round up the course,
by each writing a letter.
After a final treat of a pampering session,
to "look good and feel better"!

When times are hard
and things are particularly rough...
Just Breath. Be kind to yourself.
Remember...You. Are. Enough.

So, pull up your fighting pants ladies,
And straighten up that crown.
Let's rise from the ashes.
And be the **Fiercest Phoenix** in town.

titbits

This is the poem that kickstarted this "meraki" project. As my hubby will attest to, I am terrible at talking about my feelings. I do however get great comfort from writing them down!

A few months before I finished my active treatment, I signed up to a Marie Keating Foundation Survive and Thrive program. Logging on every Monday evening for those six weeks to chat, laugh, cry and share tips with fellow thrivers, felt like a giant warm hug. This program was instrumental to my overall recovery and helping me to make that transition to a new life after cancer. The program was exactly what I needed, at exactly the right time.

I wrote this poem directly after shutting down my laptop one night, after the penultimate weekly zoom call with my "Survive and Thrive" army. I wanted to capture all the wonderful things we had learned in just six short weeks. Something for us to look back on and draw from our "toolbox" whenever needed. Cancer is not a path anyone can walk alone, and thanks to the support of organisations such as The Marie Keating Foundation, ARC and Purple House, it's not one anyone has to.

Like so many other thrivers, my story began as a sad one, but gradually the ole humour came back. Like finding your voice again, I had again found my pen! These poems lived as scrambled notes on my phone and I figured why not take a leap of faith and share them with you, with the hopes they resonate and bring some comfort in knowing you are not alone. Hopefully this book can show that following on from a cancer diagnosis, you will thrive with empathy, humour and compassion.

This poem is for all you fabulous, fierce phoenixes out there, rising with resilience and again sparkling like the diamonds you are.

bloom
the early bird catches the worm

A beautiful garden in Bloom,
both lush and earthy.
Planted with flowers representing each stage
of a cancer survivor's journey.

Overwhelming at the start,
her brain desperately trying to focus.
The dark pink rose in the corner,
symbolising her diagnosis.

Weighed down by uncertainty,
surgeries and chemo.
The dark rose bows her head,
while her petals hang low.

Supported by loved ones,
like the trellis on the wall.
Carrying her forward on this journey,
ensuring her petals don't fall.

Hydrated by her tears
and nourished by your love.
The rose once wilting,
slowly again starts to bud.

She's come out the other side,
and treatment will be over soon.
The dark rose once withered,
slowly again starts to Bloom.

Now a vibrant pink rose,
the birds are once again singing.
Songs of peace and protection
and the hope of a new beginning.

So, just as a tiny seed grows,
into a beautiful flower.
Catching cancer early,
really is a super power.

No need to feel embarrassed,
or even to squirm.
Like the saying goes,
"The early bird catches the worm".

Drop by and visit our rose garden,
come smell its perfume.
Say hi to the Marie Keating vibrant pink roses,
here today in full Bloom.

A cancer journey may be filled
with both beauty and with sorrow.
But to plant a garden,
is to believe in tomorrow.

titbits

This poem was inspired by the Marie Keating Foundation's Garden at Bord Bia's Bloom in the Park 2023. The theme of the garden was "catching cancer early", highlighting the crucial role early detection plays in cancer survival and treatment plans. This powerful message was brought to life by the wonderfully talented designer Robert Moore. The garden went on to win gold!

I wrote this poem to capture the garden's theme, incorporating the various stages of a cancer patient's journey – from those dark days of diagnosis to the brighter days of hope and new beginnings. The poem was printed in the garden flier and the last line carved into the posts surrounding the garden.

I was invited along to Bloom as one of the Marie Keating Foundation patient ambassadors and to recite my poem at their Breakfast Briefing. This was just the most perfect way to celebrate the start of my recovery, surrounded by the Marie Keating Foundation vibrant pink roses, along with my Mum, Dad and hubby Paul.

The garden was donated to The Recovery Haven in Tralee. Robert saved a beautiful pink "lychnis petite jenny" for me. I've named her "Roberta". She has weathered a few storms but I'm happy to report that she continues to thrive and bloom!

nineteen lessons i've learned during nineteen months of treatment

1. At the start it's overwhelming and nothing seems real.
   Just trust in the process and allow yourself to feel all the feels.

2. Life delivers us lemons to serve as a reminder.
   We all need to be sounder and just a little bit kinder.

3. Eat the bar of chocolate and buy those damn shoes.
   Instead limit your intake of gloom and bad news.

4. Life can feel unfair and at times a bit rough.
   But it teaches us a good lesson, to not sweat the small stuff.

5. Cancer is not your fault, don't listen to that muck.
   It's basically some dodgy DNA and just rotten bad luck.

6. I promise you that each sad day, will again be replaced with laughter.
   Say yes to it all, you can think about it after!

7. I'm forever indebted to those, who lifted me when down.
   It goes without saying you all deserve a crown.

8. Try swopping the fast life, for a much slower pace.
    Enjoy leisurely walks in nature, instead of running the
    rat race.

9. If you are lonely or worried, just pick up the phone.
    There's always a listening ear, no one needs to walk
    this alone.

10. Family and friends (including some fluffy and hairy),
    Can make everything better and a little less scary.

11. No matter who you are or what it is that you do.
    The three most important words in the world are "I
    love you".

12. Time, not diamonds, is the commodity most precious.
    Spend it with your loved ones, their happiness is infec-
    tious.

13. Cancer gives perspective, along with clarity.
    Do what you love, making memories is key.

14. Cry for loved ones you have lost, let your tears flow.
    Tears are left over love, looking for a new place to go.

15. Enjoy the little things in life, most of them free.
    There is beauty and joy in simplicity.

16. Tomorrow is a gift, it's never just a given.
    We only get one shot at it; your life is for living.

17. Confronted with your mortality, it's natural to fear
    dying.
    Just don't let a fall, stop you from flying.

18. You have been given a second chance, "Volume 2 the remix".
Now's your time to shine, and rise like a Fierce Phoenix.

19. As the saying goes "for everything there is a season".
When it comes to a cancer diagnosis, at least we now have some rhyme, just unfortunately no reason.

little things mean a lot

A smile from a stranger.
A dog's wagging tail.
The rustling of leaves,
As the wind blows a gale.

The comfort of touch.
Holding a loved one's hand.
A day at the beach,
Toes covered in sand.

The smell of brewing coffee,
Or oven baked bread.
Hearing the words "I love you"
The first time they're said.

The crunch of thick frost.
Catching snowflakes on your tongue.
A child's hearty giggles.
Making you feel forever young.

Fresh sheets on your own bed.
A gathering with family.
Your favourite sweet left in the box.
Getting that sixth coffee for free.

Lounging in bed,
Long after its time to get up.
Happy to hurkle-durkle,
Instead of doing the wash up.

A rainbow after a storm.
A car smelling of "new".
A friendly text just to say,
"I'm thinking of you".

Kids anxiously waiting,
for Santa's magic to come.
The privilege of celebrating,
Another trip around the sun.

Life is for living,
Lest we forget.
The sun always rises
and continues to set.

I'm counting my blessings,
for all that I've got.
It's these precious little things
that mean such a lot.

titbits

Cancer definitely humbles you and teaches you to really value the little things in life. Actively seek out the simple little things every day and savor each and every little magic moment.

There is true beauty in simplicity.

author

Dearbhaile O'Hare

About me

Cancer kicker, poetry prattler.

Sales Director, photographer.

Animal lover and nature bather.

Possibly the world's wonkiest
qualified personal trainer.

Thriving, grateful, happy and hopeful.

Currently living in Dublin, but
Birr will always be my local!

illustrator

Jessica Pierce

About me

Jessica Pierce is an illustrator and a student graphic designer based in Wicklow. Working across many mediums, Jessica loves to solve problems creatively and bring a vision to life. Tackling the subject of cancer has been personal for her and she hopes to have captured some of the chaos and emotional turmoil of a positive diagnosis. Jessica is now cancer free and is feeling incredibly lucky to be pursuing her dream career.

For all enquiries
see piercedesigninfo@gmail.com

keep in touch

Be our breasties - we would love to hear from you!

thingswenttitsup
@ThingsWentTU
thingswenttitsup@gmail.com
https://www.thingswenttitsup.ie
TW TU

about the marie keating foundation

Following their mother Marie's death from breast cancer in 1998, the Keating family promised to provide the people of Ireland with vital information, advice and support on the signs and symptoms of cancer and help to prevent cancer or detect it at its earliest stages. The Marie Keating Foundation was established in her memory and with this central ambition in mind.

The Foundation's mission is to make cancer less frightening by enlightening and their aim is to live in a world free from the fear of cancer.

Originally set up to raise awareness and provide support around breast cancer, today, the Marie Keating Foundation provides information on all types of cancer and is one of the leading voices in Ireland for cancer prevention, awareness, and support.

They are committed to being there for people diagnosed with cancer, and their families at every step of a cancer journey, and their services reflect that. Through the Foundation's information and support services, they reach thousands of people every year, giving education, information and advice focused on cancer prevention and early detection, as well as providing support services and financial assistance to those living with and beyond cancer.

Their team and Board work tirelessly to ensure that the mission and legacy that the Keating Family established 25 years ago is fulfilled, and everyone in Ireland has access to trusted information on cancer prevention and early detection and that those on a cancer journey have the support they need to come through it.

For more information, please visit www.mariekeating.ie.

about purple house

Purple House is Ireland's 1st Community based Cancer Support Centre, founded in 1990. They provide professional Cancer Support & Psycho-Oncology services to people affected by Cancer. Purple House helps families affected by Cancer Nationwide in Ireland free of charge. Catering for patients, survivors, carers, families, friends and healthcare workers, people of all ages, children and adults, they help over 1,500 families each year in Ireland. A special thanks go to the team in Purple House Bray, in particular Emma Casey and Emer Ivory.

Printed in the USA
CPSIA information can be obtained
at www.ICGtesting.com
LVHW062340251223
767339LV00038B/1042